S0-AGX-371

6/20/2009

To the Filipancic's

All Good things

Jim

5 Words and Then Some:

How to Succeed In This Big Game We Call Life

by Fran Larkin

iUniverse, Inc.
New York   Bloomington

5 WORDS AND THEN SOME
How to Succeed in This Big Game We Call Life

Copyright © 2009 by Fran Larkin

All rights reserved. No part of this book may be used or reproduced by any means, graphic, electronic, or mechanical, including photocopying, recording, taping or by any information storage retrieval system without the written permission of the publisher except in the case of brief quotations embodied in critical articles and reviews.

iUniverse books may be ordered through booksellers or by contacting:

iUniverse
1663 Liberty Drive
Bloomington, IN 47403
www.iuniverse.com
1-800-Authors (1-800-288-4677)

Because of the dynamic nature of the Internet, any Web addresses or links contained in this book may have changed since publication and may no longer be valid. The views expressed in this work are solely those of the author and do not necessarily reflect the views of the publisher, and the publisher hereby disclaims any responsibility for them.

ISBN: 978-1-4401-2340-5 (pbk)
ISBN: 978-1-4401-2341-2 (ebk)

Library of Congress Control Number: 2009923040

Printed in the United States of America

iUniverse rev. date: 3/18/2009

"Around the Corner", from SELECTED POEMS by Charles Hanson Towne, copyright 1925 by D.Appleton & Co., copyright renewed 1953 by Ara Searle. Used by permission of Dutton, a division of Penguin Group (USA) Inc

This book is dedicated to my mother, who died of Alzheimer's in September 2007, and to the other five million people who have this disease. I hope we find a cure for this horrible, insidious disease in the very near future. Mom used to be a voracious reader, loved watching movies, doing crossword puzzles, cooking, traveling, and painting. She couldn't do any of that the last several years, but she did implant the Five Words in me long before that.

Contents

Acknowledgments

To Jon Barb, for all your advice, inspiration, and support. As I wrote this book, I always tried to do what works for me! Thanks for all your support, help, and inspiration. You got your book published first, but I am right behind you.

And to Patsy Tiriolo, thanks for listening and for your encouragement. You have no idea how much it meant to me.

And to my wonderful family, starting with my wife of over thirty-eight years, Kathy. I won the lottery many years ago when I married you. How I ever ended up with someone so beautiful and smart, I will never know. Someone must have been looking out for me. And to our three wonderful children, Kerry, Matt, and Leigh Ann. Being there for all of your births was an incredible experience, and seeing how you have all turned out has been even more incredible. Thanks for putting up with me all these years while I worked on this book.

Introduction

This originally started out as a small book given to my nieces and nephews when they graduated from high school. Then I expanded it to sons and daughters of close friends. The book was an attempt to share with them what I had learned in the over forty years since I graduated from high school, to help them get through the difficult transition from teenager to adult, and to increase their odds of succeeding in this great game we call life.

While originally intended for high school and/or college graduates, I realized this book applies equally to everyone, regardless of his or her stage in life. The first part of the book is called "Five Words." I have found over the years that if you apply these five words—hard work, attitude, enthusiasm, perseverance, and fun—to everything you do, you have an excellent chance of success.

The second part of the book is called "And Then Some." Once you have completed high school, college, vocational school, or the armed services, and you are applying the Five Words to everything you do, you are also going to encounter many other challenging situations in your life. "And Then Some" is full of advice, helpful hints, quotations, ideas, and miscellaneous tidbits to help you deal with those situations. "And Then Some" is based on my experiences over the past sixty years here on spaceship earth. You may never experience some of these situations in life, but if you do, here are some thoughts on how to deal with them.

So curl up in your favorite easy chair, open up the book or turn on your iPod, brew a fresh cup of coffee, and dig in! I hope you have as much fun reading the book as I did writing it.

Fran Larkin
Newburyport, Massachusetts
December, 2008

Five Words

Hard Work

Thomas Edison said, "Genius is 1 percent inspiration and 99 percent perspiration." So if you want to be a genius in life, bust your gut. There aren't too many cases of someone dying of hard work. No matter what you do and where you are, arrive early and leave late. Do you realize that if you come to work fifteen minutes early, leave fifteen minutes later, and shorten your lunchtime by fifteen minutes, you can work an extra two days a month? Even if you don't get paid for those extra hours, it will pay off down the road. And a lot of your co-workers and managers will be wondering how you get more work done than those around you, even though you appear to be on the same work schedule. Those fifteen minutes here and there add up.

Most people who have had successful careers did not work thirty-five to forty hours a week. When I look back over my thirty-five years with IBM, I worked fifty to sixty hours a week for a large portion of my career. And that includes the many nights, weekends, and travel times. One project I worked on, we called nine-seven-four. There were nine of us working seven days a week for four months. And numerous managers like to say that when they want to get something done, they give it to their busiest employee. Those employees are usually very well organized and have efficient time-management skills. But be careful here. You want to work hard. You want to get ahead. But don't neglect your family and friends. If you work late one night, leave on time the next night, and be home for dinner. If you have to do some work, do it after the kids are in bed. Make time to go to school events. Take a vacation day or half a vacation day if you have to.

And always remember, "The only way to be on time is to be early." Don't be one of those people who comes flying in the door at the last minute and then takes several minutes to get settled. And always sit in the front—in a meeting at work, in church, in a class, wherever—and always volunteer for projects and extra assignments, no matter how busy you are. I always signed up to coordinate United Way campaigns, blood drives, and other volunteer activities. I was just as busy as everyone else, but these volunteer projects were important to the community and needed to be done. Plus it was a great experience giving speeches, meeting a lot of people, and making a name for myself.

I started working when I was ten years old, mowing lawns around town and shoveling snow in the winter. In eighth grade, I broke my wrist playing rundown at Brooks Park. After I had healed a little bit, I resumed working. One lady only paid me fifty cents per hour instead of one dollar because I only had one arm. Then, I worked throughout high school in the spring, helping to take care of the grounds at Wequassett Inn in East Harwich. Baseball was my favorite sport, but I only played in eighth grade. I worked all the other years and turned in a lot of the money I earned to Dad and Mom because times were pretty tough back then.

In college, it took me five years to take four years' worth of classes, mainly because I flunked some courses, and many semesters I worked twenty to thirty hours a week in the dining commons. I didn't have to buy a meal ticket and got paid for working. One spring, I stayed on campus and cleaned the bathrooms in several of the dorms. Another spring, I worked on Glenn Rowley's cranberry bog, cleaning up all the debris and getting the bogs ready for the season. And most of the friends I had all worked at various jobs during the school year and the summer. Hard work never hurt any of us, and it instilled in us the work ethic that helped us have successful lives.

"Do more than you are asked and contribute more than is required. Go the extra mile. Remember the joy of working is seeing rainbows in thunderstorms." That's what Denis Waitley and Reni Witt assert in their book *The Joy of Working*.

And Henry Ward Beecher said, "In the ordinary business of life, industry can do anything which genius can do and make things which it cannot."

And as that great football philosopher Vince Lombardi once declared, "Luck is when preparation meets opportunity."

One person, working hard, can accomplish so much. As Helen Keller expressed, "I am only one, but still I am one. I cannot do everything, but still I can do something. I will not refuse to do the something I can do."

Archimedes had a similar thought: "Give me a place to stand, and I will move the world." Be that one—move the world!

And speaking of moving the world, Senator Robert F. Kennedy, who was assassinated in 1968 while running for president, gave a majestic, moving, and powerful speech to students at Cape Town, South Africa, and at Fordham University in 1966. Every time I read this speech, I get chills down my spine. Bobby talked about how some great men and women changed history and moved the world—and so can we all. He said, "Few will have the greatness to bend history itself, but each of us can work to change a small portion of events, and in the total of those acts will be written the history of this generation. It is from numberless diverse acts of courage and belief that human history is shaped. Each time a man stands up for an ideal, or acts to improve the lot of others, or strikes out against injustice, he sends forth a tiny ripple of hope, and crossing each other from a million different centers of energy and daring, those ripples build a current that can sweep down the mightiest walls of oppression and resistance.".

I suggest you send forth a ripple of hope from your hometown. It will create ripples of hope emanating from Danbury, Connecticut, and Harwich, Massachusetts, and Fishers Island, New York, and Chandler, Arizona, and points north, east, south, and west. Together, we will all build a current that will make spaceship earth a better place to live. Bobby Kennedy closed many of his speeches when he was campaigning with the following: "Some men see things as they are and say, why. I dream things that never were and say, why not."

Attitude

The great baseball player Reggie Jackson declared, "Whether you think you can or you think you can't, you're right!" We all have a choice when we get out of bed in the morning—we can have a positive attitude or we can have a negative attitude. Why not have a positive attitude? You will feel much better each day, and you will be healthier throughout your life. Science has now been able to confirm that there is a definite correlation between a positive attitude and health and happiness.

Throughout my career, whenever I had my annual performance appraisal, my manager would always comment on my positive attitude and the impact it had on the rest of the employees. It didn't directly affect my rating because that was based on achieving the objectives that I had at the beginning of the year, but it certainly helped my reputation. Not only did I have a reputation of getting things done, but also of doing my work in a positive, enthusiastic manner. So my positive demeanor definitely helped me in my career and my outside activities.

To quote Charles Swindoll, "The longer I live, the more I realize the impact of attitude on life. Attitude, to me, is more important than facts. It is more important than the past, than education, than money, than circumstances, than failures, than success, than what other people think, say, or do. It is more important than appearance, giftedness, or skill. It will make or break an organization, a school, a home. The remarkable thing is we have a choice each day regarding the attitude we will embrace for that day. We cannot change our past—we cannot change the fact that people will act in a certain way. We cannot change the inevitable. The only thing we can do is play on the one string we have, and that is our attitude. I am convinced that life is 10 percent what happens to me and 90 percent how I react to it." These are pretty good words to live by, every day.

We'll be talking about the five words: hard work, attitude, enthusiasm, perseverance, and fun. Well, we also should keep in mind three letters—ALL:

"A" stands for appreciation. Make sure that throughout your life, you let your parents, your friends, your neighbors, your relatives, etc. know how much you appreciate what they have done for you. It can be a simple thank you, a short note, or a quick phone call. Or just a hug and a "Thanks, Dad. Thanks, Mom. I appreciate what you have done for me."

The first "L" stands for love. Make sure you let your children, your parents, your relatives, and your spouse know how much you love them and how much they mean to you. We can't say this often enough.

The second "L" stands for laughter. Everyone loves to laugh, and people like someone who makes them laugh. Go out of your way to make others smile and laugh. You will feel better for doing it, and you will make them feel better.

The Book of Proverbs says, "As he thinketh in his heart, so is he." As you think, so you are, and so you will be. And when you get out of bed in the morning, you can think about how to have a great day or how to have a bad day. I will tell you how to have a great day. This is paraphrased from a sign that one of my co-workers had. It didn't have an author indicated, so I can't give credit, but the message is a good one. I kept it in my offices and cubes and would look at it every day:

How to Have a Great Day

Awaken Early	Appreciation for Life
Inspirational Reading	Good News Immediately
Early Morning Exercise	Vibrant Health and a Strong Body
Devotion and Thanksgiving	Recognition and Expectation
Positive Tape or CD Message	Vision and Encouragement
Shower and Readiness	Freshness and Anticipation
Have a Nourishing Breakfast	Alertness, Energy, Vitality
Multiple Vitamins	Energy, Vitality, Immunity
Wholesome, Positive Thoughts	Accomplishment and Wealth
Pleasant Greetings to Everyone	Many Friends and Happiness
Give Sincere Appreciation	Love, Honor, and Cooperation
Listen More, Talk Less	Respect, Approval, Knowledge
Plan for the Day and the Future	Creativity and Organization
Do One Task at a Time	Accomplish a Lot
See Your Work as Pleasurable	Outstanding Achievement
Have a Moderate Lunch	Alive, Alert, and Awake
Count Your Blessings	Abundance, Love, Serenity
Play and Relaxation	Happiness and Enjoyment
Moderation and Temperance	Clear, Calm, and Organized
Reasonable Dinner	Comfortable and Relaxed
Review Your Accomplishments	Peace of Mind and Success
Prayer	Homage and Self-confidence
Relax and Sleep	Sweet Dreams and a Full Life

And here's the converse:

How to Have a Lousy Day

Awaken Late/Have to Rush	Anxiety and Bitterness
Go Get the Morning Paper	Mostly Bad News
Digest Bad News on the Run	Feel Bad and Get Mad
No Devotion or Inspiration	Low Spirit, Easily Offended
No Exercise	Sluggish, Tired, Run-down
Radio or Television Reports	Disaster, Trouble, and Despair
Too Late to Shower	Sleepy, Unkempt, Smelly
No Breakfast or Just Coffee and Donut	Hungry, Grumpy, Nervous
Cigarette, Candy, Soda	Hacking Cough, Indigestion
Unfriendly and Ugly to Others	Few Friends
Criticize, Condemn, Complain	Condemnation, No Love
Dictate, Direct, and Demand	Disrespect and Ridicule
No Plans for the Day or Future	Disorganized and Sour
Tackle Everything at Once	Confusion and Disorder
See Your Job as a Necessary Evil	Barely Get By
Lunch Is Greasy, Fatty, and Rushed	Drowsy and Dull
Work, Work, Work, Work	Too Busy to Rest and Relax, Fatigued
Curse Life and Gripe	Poverty, Hate, and Worry
No Play and No Relaxation	Tension and Frustration
Indulgence and Dissipation	Illness, Tired, Little Confidence
Dinner Is Eating and Drinking Heavily	Indigestion and Poor Sleeping
Worry, Fret, and Tense	Sickness, Fear, and Failure
No Prayer or Thanksgiving	Selfish, Resentful, and Jealous
Stay Uptight and Poor Sleep	Bad Dreams and Half a Life

Boy, who wants to hang around with a person like that? I am sure we all know some people who have those attributes, and I feel badly for them. When they get out of bed, they can just as easily follow the list on how to have a good day, but they choose not to. These types of individuals can really affect an office and the morale of the people who work there. Try not to associate with these types of individuals. If you do, you could very easily end up with the same reputation as them, and this could impact your career. I worked with some people like this, and it was not fun. I did everything I could to stay away from them as much as possible.

Enthusiasm

Ralph Waldo Emerson said, "Nothing great was accomplished without enthusiasm." Approach everything you do in school, at work, with your family, and in your community with gusto. Denis Waitley and Reni Witt wrote in *The Joy of Working*, "Enthusiasm is not dependent on talent or genius or upbringing. In fact, it is enthusiasm that frequently transforms average abilities into extraordinary success."

Smile all the time. When you frown or scowl, you use over thirty muscles in your face. When you smile, you only use fourteen. Simply by smiling all the time, we will all feel better. My grandmother, Grammy Larkin, told me many years ago to always walk with my head up. Never look down and mope while you are walking somewhere. Stand up straight. Pull those shoulders back. Suck that stomach in. Always shake hands with a firm handshake and look the person in the eye. Remember, we only have one chance to make a first impression.

Also, you should try to be definitive in your answers when someone asks you a question. I was visiting my Grandfather Kee in the summer of 1961, and he asked me if I wanted another pork chop. I said, "I don't care." And he said, "Well, if you don't care, I don't care," and he never did pass that pork chop. He passed that lesson on to me because when he was a young boy growing up in North Carolina in the early 1900s, he was walking home in the pouring rain, and a friend of the family came by in a covered buckboard and horse and asked my grandfather if he wanted to get out of the rain and have a ride home. My grandfather replied, "I don't care." And the family friend said, "Well Elmore, if you don't care, I don't care." And he rode off and left my grandfather to walk home in the rain.

Always speak in a clear, audible voice. Don't ever mumble. Just as you always put energy in your walk, put energy in your voice. Be like Johnny Appleseed—spread the seeds of enthusiasm wherever you go. You will find that it is infectious.

And as the wonderful actor Tommy Lee Jones asserted, "I work at being optimistic about life. Pessimism, certainly cynicism, is an enemy. Those things destroy possibilities. Optimism is the right outlook to have. I'm convinced it creates possibilities."

Being an enthusiastic employee was another attribute that my managers would comment on in my annual appraisal. No matter what type of project I had—and some were pretty lousy—I tried to do them all in a complete, thorough manner and sought to be very enthusiastic while doing them. It made the time go by more quickly, it was easier to complete the project, and the results came out better. And yes, if I did get a lemon project, I always tried to turn it into lemonade.

Studies have shown that character, personality, work habits, and current job experience account more for success on the job than the school you graduated from. So if you follow these Five Words and become an expert in your personal profession, you have an excellent chance of succeeding in whatever job you have.

Perseverance

You will find that as you journey through life, it is not always going to be fair. You are going to get knocked down often—so you are just going to have to keep getting up. Ray Kroc, the founder of McDonald's said, "Press on. Nothing in the world can take the place of persistence. Talent will not. Nothing is more common than unsuccessful individuals with talent. Genius will not. The world is full of educated derelicts. Persistence and determination alone are omnipotent."

After I graduated from college, I started interviewing for jobs. I had over two dozen interviews before I found a job. Now to be fair, some of those interviews were just exploratory—and others, I was not interested in the job. And some, they were not interested in me. But I kept at it. Finally I had an interview with IBM. But I didn't get that job. I guess I did not do as well in the interview and the test as other candidates. But they told me they had another job, at a lower level and a lower salary: six thousand nine hundred dollars. That was *per year*, not per month. It was collecting accounts receivable. I had never heard of that, but I was getting married in a few months and needed a job, so I said I would take it. I gave it everything I had. I applied the Five Words, and within a couple of years, I was the recognized expert in collecting money in the Northeast, and I was traveling around New England giving seminars.

A few years later, I was on the list of management candidates for IBM in the northeast part of the country. I saw others get promoted before me, and I thought I was just as qualified as them. But I wished them well and just kept doing my current job the best I could. Eventually I got that promotion, which led to several other promotions over the years. Eventually I reached the highest job level you could in IBM— Senior Program Manager—which was just shy of the executive level. I was pretty proud of that. This was not bad for a kid with humble beginnings on Cape Cod.

I was doing some running in the 1970s and decided to get serious and train for the New York City marathon. I trained for a year, following a gradual buildup training guide. Two weeks before the marathon in 1981, I did my "long run" of 21 miles. I felt great and knew I was ready. I just wanted to finish in less than 4 hours. I took my time and enjoyed the race. I finished the first 13.1 miles in about 1 hour and 52 minutes. I felt great and was on target to break 4 hours. Then my right knee started killing me. I had not had any training problems other than some minor aches. My father had died the year before, so I had dedicated this race to him, and I was running with his last driver's license in my left hand. Now what do I do? I decided that because I came this far, I was going to finish, no matter how intense the pain. I ran/walked the second half of the race in just under 3 hours and finished around 4 hours and 45 minutes. I missed my goal, but I finished, in memory of Dad.

We have all heard of Michael Jordan. Did you know he tried out for his high school basketball team and was cut? Did he quit? Heck no! He went back and practiced and practiced and made the team the next year and became the best basketball player on the planet.

We have all heard of Alexander Graham Bell, the inventor of the telephone, but did you know when he tried to get financial backing for his invention, he was laughed at? Did he quit? No, he didn't. He kept at it and eventually developed an invention that has revolutionized how the world communicates.

Did you know that Winston Churchill finished last in his class, and folks thought that Walt Disney was "goofy" because he was always drawing cartoons. People wondered when he would get a real job.

Mary Higgins Clark, the Queen of Suspense, went six years and forty rejection slips before her first short story was published.

Mark Twain lost his wife, son, two daughters, a brother, and a personal fortune, but he didn't quit.

Jeff Kent, the great second baseman, tried out for his high-school baseball team all four years and never made the team. In 2000, he was the Most Valuable Player (MVP) in the National League.

Ray Charles was fifteen years old, an orphan, blind, and a black man in the South. Despite these odds, he became one of the great singers and songwriters of the twentieth century.

And the renowned chef, Emeril Lagasse, started out washing pots and pans when he was ten years old. Now he has a successful TV show, has written several books, and owns several restaurants.

Samuel L. Jackson, one of the leading actors of our generation, spent twenty years trying to land a lead role on stage and screen and also had to overcome a drug addiction.

And Bill Russell, the greatest winner in pro sports, who won eleven NBA Championships in thirteen years and finished first eighteen years out of the twenty-one that he played basketball, had to overcome racism and bigotry in his early years while playing for the Boston Celtics.

And more recently, the 2004 Boston Red Sox were down three games to none to the mighty Yankees and trailed by one run with three outs to go in game four and faced the greatest reliever in baseball history, Mariano Rivera. Not only did the Red Sox win the game, they won four straight to defeat the Yankees. No team in baseball history had ever come back from a three-game deficit.

Another great example of perseverance is Bobby Darin, one of the world's greatest entertainers. He died in 1973 at age thirty-seven. But the doctor told his mother when he was a little boy that he wouldn't live past fifteen because of the damage rheumatoid fever had done to his heart. That didn't stop him from writing one hundred sixty-three songs, recording over four hundred songs, playing seven instruments, winning two Grammy awards, getting nominated for an Academy Award as Best Supporting Actor, doing great impressions, and dancing up a storm. Along with Sammy Davis, Jr., Bobby Darin was probably the greatest entertainer in show business history. That's not bad for someone who was supposed to die at fifteen.

We recently celebrated the sixtieth anniversary of Jackie Robinson's first baseball game in the Major Leagues on April 15, 1947. How he endured what he went through and how he put up with all the slurs, taunting, insults, etc., I will never know. What an example of perseverance for all of us.

And how about this as an example of perseverance: He lost his job. He was defeated for the legislature. He failed in business. He was elected to the legislature. His girlfriend died. Then he suffered a nervous breakdown. He was defeated for Speaker of the state legislature. He was defeated for nomination to Congress. He was elected to Congress. He lost his renomination to Congress. He was rejected for the position of land officer. He was defeated for the Senate. He was defeated for the nomination of Vice President. He was defeated for the Senate, again. He was elected the sixteenth president of the United States—Abraham Lincoln. As it did for Old Abe, victory will surely come to those of us who make a habit of perseverance.

I have given several examples of perseverance because, out of all the Five Words, I think this is the most important and the one that played the biggest role in the success I have had in life. During my college years and the early years at work, this kept me going. I would not quit. I would not give up. I hung in there. And it all worked out.

Fun

We are all going to be dead for a long time, so we should have fun living now. Enjoy the ride! Have fun along the way and learn to laugh often and also to laugh at yourself. Take your studies, your job, and your family seriously, but never take yourself too seriously.

And always remember, there is no documented record of anyone on his or her deathbed saying, "I should have spent more time at the office." Make time for your family and yourself. Get to your kid's plays, recitals, basketball games, and school meetings. Make sure you get home for dinner with the family as often as you can. And don't live to work. Work to live. Christopher Marley said, "There is only one success—to be able to spend your life in your own way." Make sure you do that and have fun doing it.

Eat an ice-cream cone. Have even two scoops. Have a candy bar. Do something spontaneous. Roll down the window of your car and play a Rolling Stones CD really loudly. If you want to live a joyous life that's full of fun, you should act joyfully. And one way to do that is to always laugh.

Ralph Waldo Emerson said, "To laugh often and much; to win the respect of intelligent people and the affection of children; to earn the appreciation of honest critics and endure the betrayal of false friends; to appreciate beauty; to find the best in others; to leave the world a bit better, whether by a healthy child, a garden patch, or a redeemed social condition; to know even one life has breathed easier because you lived. This is to have succeeded."

My motto at work was, "To work hard, make the numbers, and have fun doing it." You can be in business and have fun. It's not all serious. You can laugh and joke and smile while working—and still get the job done! I used to participate in all the sales meetings we had. Boy, were those fun. One year, the theme was "The train to New Orleans." So for our kickoff meeting, we rented an entire railroad for the day. Another time, we brought a live cow up to the second floor. I forget who had to clean up afterward.

I would also get involved in the writing and performing of skits. Over the years, I would be many of the characters from the Johnny Carson show—Carnac, Aunt Blabby, and more. The meetings increased the morale, improved the camaraderie, reduced the stress and strain that everyone was under, and were just plain fun.

Numerous studies have shown that offices and work groups that have a friendly, positive, and enthusiastic atmosphere are more productive, get more done, and have less personnel problems. Make sure you incorporate this in your business environment.

Spelling Game

Here's a little spelling game:

Take the S from Perseverance

The U from Fun

The C from Perseverance

The C from Enthusiastic

The E from Attitude

The S from Enthusiastic

The second S from Enthusiastic

Place them all on a foundation of hard work and here's what you get:

SUCCESS!

And Then Some

Quotations

On many occasions, we will find ourselves in a situation where a good quote will come in handy. Maybe it's at a promotion party for someone at work, or maybe it's a retirement party, or a dinner with some friends, or maybe it's a birthday party for a family member. Here are some quotes that have worked for me over the years.

"We are what we repeatedly do. Excellence, then, is not an act, but a habit." —Aristotle (Good to share with whomever you work with or manage.)

"If we don't change our direction, we might end up where we're headed." —Chinese proverb (Good to use kicking off a planning session.)

"Grow old with me for the best is yet to be." —Robert Browning

"Think where man's glory most begins and ends, and say my glory was I had such friends." —Yeats

"A father is a treasure, a brother is a comfort, but a friend is both." —Ben Franklin (The above two quotes are good to use if you are going out to dinner with friends and you want to make a toast. Instead of just saying "cheers," you can use the above.)

"This is not the end. This is not even the beginning of the end. It is indeed the end of the beginning." —Churchill (This is good to use when writing a note to someone who is leaving a job, retiring, etc. You can use the quote and then say something to the effect of, "Good luck as you begin the next phase of your life.")

"Be the change you seek." —Gandhi

"The dogmas of the quiet past will not work in the turbulent future. As our cause is new, so must we think and act anew." —Abraham Lincoln (This is good to use when you are gathering a team to work on a project and you are kicking off the meeting.)

"Shoot for the moon, and if you miss, you will still land amongst the stars." —Unknown (This is good to use when talking to a group of graduates.)

"Thanking you for your time, this time, until next time." —Unknown

"I'll talk and you listen. If you get done before me, raise your hand." —Unknown

"Thank you for that applause. It is twice as much as I deserved, but only half as much as I expected." —Unknown

Bishop Fulton J. Sheen, a Catholic priest who had a television show in the 1950s, used to say that if you applauded for someone before they spoke, that was a sign of faith; if you applauded while they spoke, that was a sign of hope; and if you applauded when they were done, that was a sign of charity. So thanks for showing a sign of faith. (The above three quotes are a good way to start off a meeting. These statements would get everyone laughing and put them in a good mood.)

"Always do the right thing. You will gratify some of the people and astonish all the rest." —Mark Twain (This is good advice to give anyone, anytime.)

"Trust in God. Believe in yourself. Dare to dream." —Robert Schuler

"May the best of your past be the worst of your future." —Unknown (This is good to use at a wedding or special event. It is short, easy to say, and profound at the same time.)

"Never have so many owed so much, to so few." —Churchill (This is great to use when you are presenting an award or plaque to a group of folks who have worked on a special project or worked overtime to get something done, etc.)

These are just a few of the numerous quotes that can be helpful. Also, use some of the quotes in the Five Words section. There are also a lot of sites on the Internet that list inspirational quotes. I like to search the discount shelves of the bookstores and look for books on quotes. I have picked up several in this matter and keep them on my bedside table.

Here is a poem that Tip O'Neill, the former Speaker of the House, used to read each year when the old gang from his neighborhood in Cambridge, Massachusetts, got together to remember the old times. After a night of storytelling, good food, and good drink, he used to close with this poem by Charles Hanson Towne, called *Around the Corner*.

Around the corner I have a friend
In this great city that has no end.
Yet days go by and weeks rush on,
And before I know it, a year is gone,

And I never see my old friend's face,
For life is a swift and terrible race.
He knows I like him just as well
As in the days when I rang his bell

And he rang mine.

We were younger then
And now we are busy, tired men;
Tired with playing a foolish game,
Tired with trying to make a name.

'Tomorrow' I say, 'I will call on Jim,
Just to show that I'm thinking of him.'
But tomorrow comes and tomorrow goes,
And the distance between us grows and grows.

Around the corner!—Yet miles away ...
'Here's a telegram, sir.
Jim died today.'

And that's what we get and deserve in the end
Around the corner, a vanished friend.

I quoted this at my twenty-fifth anniversary at work. It's a major milestone. IBM gives you a nice lunch, presents, and a book of letters from your peers. After the lunch, it's a tradition to have everyone go around the table and say something about you. Sometimes it's serious, and sometimes it's a mini-roast.

After everyone was done talking, I read this quote, and there were a lot of tears flowing. I closed by saying to everyone that we have to stay in touch and we don't want to get any telegrams.

This proves to be pretty powerful stuff.

Meetings

If I had a dime for every meeting I have been to in the last thirty-five years, I would probably be a millionaire. But if I had a dime for every effective meeting I have been to, I would be lucky to be able to buy a cup of coffee.

We are all going to attend a lot of meetings in our lifetimes—at work, in the community, in school, in the service, or in church. Here are a few guidelines to run an effective meeting, whether four people are going to attend or more than forty. (For more details, the library, bookstores, and the Internet have books and articles on how to run a meeting.)

Send out a reminder and an agenda, either via e-mail or regular mail, several days in advance.

Get there early and check out the room to make sure it is set up properly—it's clean, there are enough chairs, etc.

Start the meeting on time. Don't wait for any laggards. It is inconsiderate for all those who showed up on time. And don't spend any time updating the latecomers.

If there are attendees who don't know each other, make sure you have introductions at the beginning of the meeting.

Cover the purpose of the meeting—what you hope to accomplish— and review the agenda.

One person should moderate and run the meeting.

Keep the meeting on track, involve everyone, and make it as much fun as possible.

Summarize the next steps and action items and who owns them at the end of the meeting.

End the meeting on time.

No meeting should be more than one hour long. After that, no one pays attention.

Send out minutes right after the meeting and include the date and time of the next meeting if there is a follow-up.

While the meeting is going on, using cell phones, pagers, and laptops should not be allowed. They are rude.

And most of all, remember that the only way to be on time is to be early.

Most meetings are really about the team in attendance—whether at work, school, church, or in the community. That team is assembled there for a purpose. You may end up having one meeting or many. Here are "Eleven Commandments for an Enthusiastic Team," by Ian Percy. I used this before every meeting that would involve a series of meetings or a project.

Help each other be right—not wrong.

Look for ways to make new ideas work—not for reasons they won't.

If in doubt, check it out. Don't make negative assumptions about each other.

Help each other win, and take pride in each other's victories.

Speak positively about each other and about your organization at every meeting.

Maintain a positive mental attitude no matter what the circumstances.

Act with initiative and courage as if it all depends on you.

Do everything with enthusiasm—it's contagious.

Whatever you want, give it away.

Don't lose faith; never give up.

Have fun.

© *The Ian Percy Corporation. Reprinted with permission. Ian Percy is a leading business speaker, consultant and author. For further information go to www.IanPercy.com*

Holidays

I think many of us have forgotten why we are celebrating holidays and what their true meaning is. I know we all live busy lives and we can all use the extra day off, but I think we have to pause—at least for a few minutes—during each holiday, and focus on why and what we are celebrating. And we can do this privately, or if you have several people over for a party, you can say a few words. Here are some of my thoughts for a few holidays. Depending on your heritage, your religion, and your background, you may have others.

Martin Luther King, Jr.'s Birthday

I reflect here on all the horrible things African-Americans have gone through in this country and what a symbol of hope Martin Luther King was and is today. Things are getting better, but we still have a long way to go when it comes to how we treat each other. I also think of everything the Native Americans went through, how Americans of Japanese descent were interred in World War II and lost their businesses and homes. And it never ceases to amaze me that women couldn't vote until 1920.

President's Weekend

While this is mainly about Lincoln and Washington, I think about all the difficult decisions these men have made, especially during times of great national crisis. Thank God that we usually have had the right person in office when tough times arrive. Franklin Roosevelt literally gave his life to save us during World War II. If he hadn't been in office making decisions, who knows what would have happened. I read somewhere that all Americans should get down on their knees and say a prayer to him for saving us. When I was at Hyde Park, I did exactly that in front of his grave.

St. Patrick's Day

I think of not only what my ancestors went through in Ireland and when they first arrived here in the United States, but I think of all immigrant groups and what they experienced to assimilate themselves into the American culture. They sure endured a lot. Plus in Boston it's Evacuation Day, which is when the British left Boston. On March 17, 1776, the British saw all the cannons mounted on Dorchester Heights and Charleston and retreated. Henry Knox led a team of hardy patriots from Fort Ticonderoga in New York to Boston, carrying almost sixty cannons on sleds in the cold and snow, in a journey that took six weeks in the middle of the winter.

Patriot's Day

This is another Massachusetts holiday, and it's celebrated on April 19 each year, commemorating that day in 1775 and the battles of Lexington, Concord, and Arlington. Lexington was where the Revolution started when eight American militia were killed on the Green; Concord was the North Bridge and "the shot heard round the world" sounded there; Arlington was another battle on that same day the British retreated toward Boston. This is when the British realized the patriots were serious and not just a bunch of rabble-rousers.

Memorial Day

I think of the hundreds of thousands of soldiers who have gone over that hill in the past two hundred years and have not come back. So many were deprived of getting married, having kids and seeing them grow up, spending holidays with family, having a cookout in the back yard, just sitting outside, having a beer, and watching the garden grow. That was truly the ultimate sacrifice.

Fourth of July

When I was growing up, every Fourth of July, Dad would take out the shotgun, load it with buckshot, go out on the back steps, point the gun in the direction of the woods, toward the police station, and fire off a round to celebrate the Fourth. This was always one of his favorite holidays, and I think of him now every Fourth of July, and I think about what an incredible group of men our founding fathers were. The Declaration of Independence will be around and discussed for hundreds of years.

Labor Day

These days, I think of all the jobs that are being outsourced to other continents, how medical benefits are being cut, pensions are being eliminated or changed in midstream to the employees' disadvantage, all the layoffs being made to make companies "more profitable," and how the people that are left have to do the work of those who were laid off. I have always believed that you cannot have delighted customers without delighted employees. Take care of your employees, and they will jump through hoops for you. And companies will still make a nice profit.

Columbus Day

We all know that Columbus really didn't "discover" America. The Native Americans were here for thousands of years, and the Vikings sailed to North America hundreds of years before Columbus. But I think of what must have been on his mind when he left Europe with the Nina, Pinta, and Santa Maria and sailed west without really knowing what was out there. And all the other explorers like Magellan, Vasco de Gama, Cortez, DeSoto, etc. How could they all leave their families, sail into the uncharted waters, and be away from home for years? Simply incredible. And I also think of how they treated the different races they found in the "New World." It was pretty horrible.

Thanksgiving

I think of everything I am thankful for—and that is quite a lot. I also think of the Pilgrims leaving Europe in September, arriving on Cape Cod in November, before finally settling in Plymouth, with winter coming on. Half of them would die the first winter, and the rest would not have survived if it had not been for the Native American, Squanto. He had been to Europe several times before he walked into the Pilgrim settlement in 1621 and taught them how to grow crops, hunt, and survive in New England. They would not have survived if it were not for him. He is buried somewhere along the shores of Pleasant Bay on Cape Cod, near my old hometown of Harwich.

I also think about what the Native Americans felt when they saw all those white sails start showing up on the horizon during the 1500s and 1600s. Did they know that their civilization would be almost gone in two hundred years? An entire race almost disappeared.

Christmas

I think of how commercial the season has become and wonder how it got this way. How did the Three Wise Men bringing presents to Jesus turn into this? And I think of the baby Jesus and wonder what exactly went on back then. And whatever you believe, something did happen there, and this poem from an unknown source that runs every year at Christmas in the local paper captures that spirit.

One Solitary Life

"He was born in an obscure village, the child of a peasant woman. He grew up in still another village, where he worked in a carpentry shop until he was thirty. Then for three years he was an itinerant preacher. He never wrote a book. He never held an office. He never had a family or owned a house. He didn't go to college. He never visited a big city. He never traveled two hundred miles from the place he was born. He did none of the things one usually associates with greatness.

"He had no credentials but himself. He was only thirty-three when the tide of public opinion turned against him. His friends ran away. He was turned over to his enemies and went through the mockery of a trial. He was nailed to a cross between two thieves. While he was dying, his executioners gambled for his clothing, the only property he had on earth. When he was dead, he was laid in a borrowed grave through the pity of a friend. Nineteen centuries have come and gone, and today he is the central figure of the human race and the leader of mankind's progress.

"All the armies that ever marched, all the navies that ever sailed, all the parliaments that ever sat, all the kings that ever reigned, put together, have not affected the life of man on this earth as much as that *one solitary life.*"

Pretty amazing and powerful stuff.

Public Speaking

Someone once said that most Americans fear speaking in public more than they fear death. There are many great books out there about public speaking, but I would like to share with you a few hints that have worked for me.

First of all, know your subject and be yourself. That's it in a nutshell. And don't think of yourself as a public speaker. What are they going to do to us when we are making a speech or giving a talk—shoot us? Of course not. And here is something else: a large portion of the people are not even listening to you. They may be looking at you, but they are thinking about what they are going to have for dinner or how they are going to pay their bills or when the next break is.

Don't try to be something you're not. Don't start off a talk with a joke if you are not good at telling jokes or if there is no purpose for telling a joke. Oftentimes, the best way to start a talk or presentation is with a quotation that is related to what you are talking about. Then lead into the talk or presentation. Always try to give the audience some value. And focus on only two or three points to make during your presentation.

And like we talked about in the chapter titled "Meetings," you still have to be prepared. You have to have your notes ready—don't ever memorize. You have to practice. You should get to the room ahead of time and make sure the podium and visuals are set up (if you use them). I try not to use a podium. I roam all over the place and use a conversational style. I use different gestures and vary my vocal delivery, and I am very spontaneous, as well. These performance aspects have worked well for me.

Also, don't come across as an expert. Be humble and make fun of yourself. And the best way to get experience is to speak in public as much as you can. Coordinate blood drives and United Way campaigns at work. That way you have to talk to groups of people. Be a lector at church. Join a Toastmasters Club. Say grace at Thanksgiving dinners. Give eulogies at funerals of friends or family members. Give a toast when out to dinner with family or friends. Read some books on public speaking, or take a course at your local college, and give talks to community groups on a subject you have some experience with.

And always remember what Bob Talbot, who was the Vice President of Quality at the IBM Credit Corporation, told me many years ago: "The Three B's—Be Good, Be Brief, Be Gone."

Twenty-five Things to Do Before You Check Out

I waited until I was fifty to start compiling this list even though I kept things in my head for years. But *you* don't have to wait until you're fifty. Start writing things down that you want to achieve and complete when you are in your teens, twenties, or whenever. Add to the list, delete items, prioritize them, reprioritize them, etc. To help get you started, here are some of the items I am working on.

Visit Gettysburg, Bull Run, Shiloh, and Antietam battlefields
Go to Normandy and stand on Omaha Beach
Run the New York City marathon again
Run the Boston Marathon
Recreate part of the Lewis and Clark expedition
Hike the Appalachian Trail
Have lunch with Mike Barnicle, Doris Kearns Goodwin, Bill James, and Chris Matthews
Visit the Field of Dreams in Iowa
Visit the Surf Ballroom in Clear Lake, Iowa
Stand on the rim of the Grand Canyon
Stand in the Oval Office and just take it all in for ten minutes
Spend several days in Las Vegas
Tour Europe and see all the battlefields from WWI and WWII

Bike across Iowa
See the OK Corral in Tombstone
Stand next to the Vietnam Memorial
Visit the Holocaust Memorial
Visit the graves of all the Presidents
Visit Ireland and see where all the Larkins came from
Travel to Italy, Greece, France, and England
Take the train all the way across Canada
Spend several days in Washington DC, taking in all the sites
Watch a baseball game at every Major League park
Visit the Negro League Hall of Fame in Kansas City
Watch the full moon come out over the ocean at Nauset Beach on Cape Cod
Have lunch with the *Extreme Makeover: Home Edition* design team
Cook a meal with Bobby Flay and Emeril Lagasse
Hike Mt. Kilimanjaro
Complete the Mt. Washington Road Race
Write a book

Make Time for Yourself

We all lead pretty hectic lives these days. In many families, both parents work while having to juggle the exhaustion that comes with long commutes, children's activities, long hours, maybe two jobs, visiting family members, etc. But we have to learn to make time for ourselves. Read or exercise or volunteer, and if you have more time, get some hobbies. There is a smorgasbord of activities out there to get involved in. I have so many hobbies, I retired so I can work on them.

I have known some people who won't retire because they don't know what to do with their time. They say to me, "How many papers can I read a day?" "How many tomato plants can I grow in the summer?" I feel so bad for them because all they really know is work and their families. They only have a few interests.

Don't get into that situation. Take up woodworking, painting, photography, cooking, dancing, running, swimming, biking, fishing, reading, hiking, or kayaking. And that's just the tip of the iceberg.

Whatever you do, as I said earlier, make sure you "work to live," not "live to work." Remember, there is no written or oral record of anyone saying as they lay on their deathbed, "I should have spent more time at the office." Keep work and home/family in balance.

So don't get stuck in a rut. Make time for yourself.

Volunteering

"We are prone to judge success by the index of our salaries or the size of our automobiles rather than by the quality of our service and relationship to mankind." Martin Luther King, Jr.

Albert Einstein was asked the purpose of human life. He said, "Why, it must be to serve others. What other purpose could there be?"

We all take a lot out of life, and I think we all have not only an obligation but a responsibility to give something back to our community. There is no better way of doing that than by volunteering in your hometown. The local paper in Danbury, Connecticut, has a section every Thursday about volunteer opportunities, and this section takes up a quarter of a page. There is something there for everyone, for every schedule, for every background and talent: drive the elderly on errands; serve food with Meals on Wheels, food pantries, or soup kitchens; give blood; tutor; answer phones for a nonprofit agency; play bingo with seniors; visit the homebound; translate documents. Homeless shelters need help. Big Brother and Big Sister programs need help. Most town halls have all kinds of committees that they need volunteers to participate in. And there is the PTA or scouts. You get the idea. There are many ways to volunteer. Get involved. Make a difference.

The great Civil War General, Robert E. Lee, taught at Washington University after the war, right up until his death in 1870. After he died, it became Washington and Lee University. He told his students that "The great duty of life is to see to the happiness and welfare of our fellow man." He believed that the greatest good was selflessness and that the greatest evil was selfishness.

Here is a quote by John Hall that captures the essence of volunteering and helping each other. I have used this when coordinating United Way Campaigns at work and speaking to various departments urging them to participate: "As you close your eyes in slumber, do you think that God will say, 'You have earned one more tomorrow by the work you did today?'"

Let's all do something "to tame the savageness of man and make gentle the life of this world."

Reading

Former Prime Minister of Israel, Shimon Peres, said, "I know there are good books and bad books. It can be fiction or nonfiction. It can be philosophy. It can be history. Really, when it comes to books, it is its value, its depth. You make an acquaintance with a book as you do with a person. After ten or fifteen pages, you know with whom you have to deal. When you have a good book, you really have something of importance. Books are as important as friends and maybe more so. Because all of us are living in very limited circles, books enable us to run away from them."

President Truman's daughter, Margaret, was once asked what her father's definition of heaven was. She said something to the effect that it was having a stack of new history or biography books on the table, next to his favorite chair. I would second that comment and just add having that chair in front of the fireplace.

I don't know what I would do if I could not read. I am amazed at the number of people I know who don't read books and who say they just don't have the time. Many of them don't read newspapers or one of the weekly news magazines. I believe we have an obligation to be informed citizens, and we have to know a little bit of what is going on in our town, state, country, and around the world.

When we go to Maine for vacation in the summer, we usually rent a cottage on a lake. One of my favorite things to do is to go up to the drugstore each morning and buy several papers and then come back to the cottage and have a few cups of coffee and read all the papers on the dock that overlooks the lake. It doesn't get any better than having the *Boston Globe, USA Today, The New York Times,* and the Portland paper at your side.

Another tradition we have before we go on vacation is to load up on books. I usually read adventure-thriller books on vacation, and I usually read about six in a two-week time. During the rest of the year, I read a lot of history and biography books. Someone once said there is no such thing as history. There is just biography. There is nothing like reading a new biography of a great American.

We all waste so much time each week, and as a nation we watch too much television. Keep a book by your bedside table and read fifteen to thirty minutes each night before you go to sleep, and read a few hours during the weekend. You will be surprised at how many books you can finish this way. I read at least a couple dozen books a year this way.

Finance

Recent Treasury Department figures indicate that approximately seventy-five million Americans have no savings or very little savings at all. No pension, no retirement savings, no 401K, no IRA's, no nothing. We have many problems here in the United States, and I think the lack of savings we have and the amount of consumer debt we carry have reached a crisis point. There are many helpful financial books out there, and I encourage you to go to the library or your favorite bookseller and read them. But to get you started on a savings plan, I am going to give you four words of financial advice—*save for yourself first*.

It is very easy to fall into the trap of paying all your bills first and then—if there is anything left—to put that leftover money into savings. And guess what? Most days there won't be anything left. Retirement may seem like it is decades away and you will have many years to figure out your savings, but it doesn't work that way. You have to start now, whether you are making ten thousand, fifty thousand, or one hundred thousand dollars. *Start now*.

Take 10 percent of your salary right off the top and put it into your company's savings plan—a 401K, an IRA, your company's stock plan, or whatever. We all waste money each month. You will find that you will get used to living on what's left, and you will get by. And you won't be eating dog food either. If you start doing this in your twenties, you will have plenty of savings by the time you reach fifty-five, sixty, or sixty-five.

The current US savings rate is something like 0.6 percent of our salaries—less than 1 percent. We just have to do better. Also, because we are all living longer, there's an even bigger need to start early. And you can't just rely on your company's plans. They can change, get reduced, or even eliminated. Make sure you don't put all your eggs into one basket. Save money in a 401K, IRA, stocks, bonds, etc.

Richard McKenzie, coauthor of *Getting Rich in America: Eight Simple Rules for Building a Fortune and a Satisfying Life,* says that becoming rich in the United States is a choice. If we choose to work hard, save prodigiously, and invest for the long haul, we are going to wake up one morning with more wealth than we could have ever imagined. And coauthor Dwight R. Lee asserts, "Most people want to get rich so that they can have a comfortable life. But, if anything, things work the opposite. If you lead a good life—a responsible life—and put in productive effort, then you will get rich." These are pretty good words to follow, and you can start by *saving for yourself first.*

And to complement saving for yourself first, try to follow some of these tips that will free up more money to live on each day: bring your lunch to work several days a week; bring your own thermos of coffee or tea bags; drink water instead of buying soft drinks; eat an apple in the afternoon instead of buying a candy bar. Just doing these few things will save close to two thousand dollars each year. And if you invest that money for forty years in a fund that makes 5 percent per year, you will have two hundred sixty-seven thousand dollars! When you invest wisely, it adds up.

Diversity

In our lives, we are all going to meet and interact with all kinds of people, from different religions, different ethnic backgrounds, and different walks of life. We are going to meet them at work, when we shop, when we travel, wherever we go. I came across this list several years ago, and I kept it in my three-ring binder at work and referred to it often. As far as I can tell, the original source was Donella Meadows, a professor at Dartmouth College. It came out around 1990 and was called "State of the Village." It has been modified since then, and the percentages may have changed a little bit on some of the items, but the message is the same.

"If we could shrink the earth's population of well over 6 billion people to a village of 100 people, and keep all the human ratios the same, this village would be made up of:

60 Asians

12 Europeans

13 people from the Western Hemisphere (North and South)

14 Africans

70 would be nonwhite, and 30 would be white

67 would not be Christian, and 33 would be Christian

15 would be illiterate

20 would suffer from malnutrition and would be dying of starvation

20 would consume 80 percent of the village's energy

20 have no clean, safe water to drink

And only 1 would have a college education

This proves the need for all of us to show tolerance, compassion, and understanding in all that we do.

Physical Fitness and Diet

USA Today recently had an article that said that 64.5 percent of all Americans are overweight and that 30 percent of us are obese—more than 30 pounds overweight. In the early 1960s, we were 42 percent overweight. We are all getting fat, and we have to do something about it. The health risks to us and the costs to the health and insurance industries are just incredible with this amount of corpulence.

I have a sister-in-law and brother-in-law who lived in Hong Kong while on an assignment for his job. And every time they flew back to the States and landed at LAX, they were amazed at the size of all the Americans they saw. We are becoming a nation of Goodyear Blimps.

I love to talk about food, I love to cook it, and I love to eat it. But why does everything have to taste so good? It is a constant battle to fight the battle of the bulge. And right now, I have the Dunlap disease—my belly is done lapping over my belt. I recently went a year and a half without eating any candy at all and dropped thirty pounds. Now I have fallen off the wagon, and I have put some of that back on. It's a constant battle. People are always bringing candy and doughnuts and cookies to work. All of our holidays are predicated on what the food is going to be first, and what is coming later.

I have gone up and down over the years. I have been Fat Fran and just regular, weigh-what-you–should-for-your-height Fran. And the secret to weighing what I should is *to eat in moderation.* That's it! You don't have to go on any special diets and waste tons of money buying the latest diet-fad book. Just do everything in moderation. Don't go without dessert, but have it once a week—not every night. And when you have cookies, have one or two, not ten or twelve. Have an ice cream once in a while, but get a small one. It doesn't have to be a triple-decker coated with heaps of Jimmies. And eat lots of fresh fruit, vegetables, fish, pasta, and salads. And wash it down with lots of water and juices. Be careful with all the diet drinks. There are no calories, but there are lots of chemicals in them.

And watch all the fast food. It tastes great, but it has tons of calories and many grams of fat. If you love a tasty, juicy steak like I do, just have one every now and then. Make it a special treat, and it will even taste better. And eat as much organic fruits, vegetables, meats, fish, and eggs as possible. And watch out for all the trans fats and saturated fats. Eat lots of whole grains.

And we all can't just eat in moderation to keep the weight down. We have to fit some exercise in, too, to keep the old body limber. I think a lot of us have health problems because we are not in shape, and the body and muscles atrophy from lack of use. We don't need a lot of fancy exercise equipment to stay in shape and keep the weight down. Our basements are filled with unused exercise bikes, Nordic Tracs, rowing machines, etc. And we don't have to join Health Clubs, either.

The secret is to join *the earth gym*. That's right, the earth gym. By this, I mean do everyday things to stay fit: park your car at the far end of the parking lot at the mall and then walk to the main entrance; walk the stairs up and down at work and don't take the elevator; if you have a yard, rake the leaves with a rake and not a blower; shovel snow whenever you can; cut wood with a bow saw and not a chain saw; if you have a garden, rake, hoe, shovel, and bend over and weed, and don't use a big, fancy tiller; mow the lawn with a push mower so you get some walking in.

We are all busy and live hectic lives, but on average we watch four to five hours of television a day. Can't we spare thirty to forty-five minutes a day just to walk? If we, as a nation, did nothing else for exercise, except that, we would lose billions of pounds, get in shape, stay in shape, save billions of healthcare costs, and live a lot longer.

So there you have it. *Eat moderately, eat better, and join the earth gym.*

Inspirational Books

There are many, many self-help and inspirational books, and I have read my share. They are all good, and each one has its own message that can make a difference in your life. The ones listed below have had the most impact on me. Here they are, in no particular order:

The Power of Positive Thinking, Norman Vincent Peale
How to Win Friends and Influence People, Dale Carnegie
How to Stop Worrying and Start Living, Dale Carnegie
Think and Grow Rich, Napoleon Hill
Seeds of Greatness, Denis Waitley
Success Through a Positive Mental Attitude, Napoleon Hill and W. Clement Stone
The Joy of Working, Denis Waitley and Reni L. Witt
Do What Works, Jon Barb
Enthusiasm Makes the Difference, Norman Vincent Peale
The Joy of Not Working, Ernie J. Zelinski
Russell Rules, Bill Russell with David Falkner
Create Your Own Future, Brian Tracy
Change Your Thinking, Change Your Life, Brian Tracy
Black Like Me, John Howard Griffin
After Jackie, Cal Fussman
Life's a Campaign, Chris Matthews

Pick up a copy of one of these books at your favorite bookseller or at your local library. Keep it on your bedside table and carry it with you and read a few pages whenever you get a free moment. Read them all and then read them again. I have read most of the above books several times. Each time you reread them, a new message will jump out at you and help you improve your life.

Your Own Mission Statement, Vision, and Values

As I said in an earlier chapter, there is an old Chinese Proverb that says, "If we don't change our direction, we might end up where we're headed." We all need to know what direction we are going to take in life and how we are going to get there. And with the decline in values and ethics in this country, we all need to take a position on what we stand for and what we believe in. Here are some techniques to help you get started. A lot of successful businesses use what I call "The Vision Thing."

Vision	How do you want to be perceived by your family, friends, neighbors and fellow workers?
Values	What do you believe in? What are your ethics? What is your moral compass?
Mission	What is your purpose here on Spaceship Earth?
Goals	What do you want to accomplish this year and long term, say the next 10 years?
Strategies	How are you going to achieve those short-term and long-term goals?
Measurements	How are you tracking towards those goals? What have you completed and what has to be done?
Critical Success Factors	What are the key things that are essential to carry out the strategies?

Heat up a cup of coffee, a pot of tea, or a mug of hot chocolate, think about the seven topics above, and write them down. Go back a few days later, look them over, and rewrite them again if necessary. And put them on one piece of paper, keep this one page in a common spot, and review it regularly. Try arranging the seven topics in a pyramid, with Vision at the top, and the others in the same order as above. If you need any help or have questions, send me an e-mail, and I will be glad to help. This is a powerful tool that helps you crystallize and focus who you are, what you believe in, and what you want to do in life.

Marriage/Relationships

When I retired from IBM in December of 2004, as was custom, my manager hosted a luncheon for me and my spouse and several of my friends from work. During lunch, the guests went around the table and said something about me, and then I said something about them. I saved the best for last. I said that I was very proud of my thirty-five-year career with IBM and what I had accomplished—but that I was even more proud of thirty-five years of being happily married and that any success I had at work was due to my wife, Kathy. She stayed home with the three kids and took care of the house and all the finances while I was working a lot of hours and traveling. So to show my appreciation for everything she had done, I reached down under the table and took out a long box and presented her with thirty-six red roses, one for each year at IBM and one for the future. Then I said thanks to her and gave her a big kiss.

The reason I told this story is because I believe we have to appreciate our spouses in order to make our marriages successful. We have to thank them for what they have done, tell them they look nice when they dress up (and even when they don't dress up), remember anniversaries, be at their sides during good times and bad, support each other, love each other, respect each other's opinions (even if you don't always agree), help out with the chores and the food shopping and cleaning, go out to eat once in while, get out of the house, and enjoy each other.

And think about those vows we all took during that special day. Try to honor, love, and cherish your spouse—in good times and bad, in sickness and health, until death do you part.

Post September 11

A few days after September 11, I was instant messaging with our youngest daughter, Leigh Ann, who was a sophomore at the University of New Hampshire at the time. Like all of us, she had many concerns about what was going to happen in the United States and around the world. I tried to reassure her that things would be OK. For some reason, I saved and printed out our conversation. Listed below is an edited version. I think the subjects we discussed applied then, and they apply to us now, too. Some of the comments are covered in other sections of this book, but I think this provides a nice summary of many of them and puts a lot of things in perspective. I also realized that I was paraphrasing a lot of what Bobby Kennedy said in his wonderful "Work of Our Hands" speech, also known as "Day of Affirmation,"—a speech that has had a significant impact on me and that I talked about earlier.

Dad: "Hi, Leigh. How are you doing? It has been a tough week for the U.S. Are you and your friends doing OK?"
Leigh: "Yes, I guess. So what do you think will happen?"
Dad: "Say some prayers for all the folks who have died and for what their families are going through. I think many things will happen on the military front over time. We will probably send ground troops into Afghanistan, send fighter jets to attack targets in several countries, and do a lot of clandestine things behind the scenes to wipe out the terrorists."

Leigh: "So what does that all mean?"

Dad: "It means that there is going to be some type of prolonged war against these creeps. It is going to last months. We could see body bags of American soldiers coming home on the evening news. The economy could slide into a recession, and flying is going to be a lot different. We will also need to tighten up a lot of things here in the U.S. Hopefully this is the end of terrorist attacks in this country."

Leigh: "Yeah, it better be. Is the stock market going to go back up from what it is today, or will it keep going down?"

Dad: "The stock market *will* go up again. We will rebuild the Twin Towers, life will continue in this country. We will persevere. Think of those school kids down south who made peanut-butter-and-jelly sandwiches and sent them to the firemen and policemen in NYC. But you cannot lose hope. Focus on the goodness in us that is being displayed in NYC by all the volunteers there and all around the country—and by all those people who drove to NYC to help just because they felt they had to be there. Think of the tremendous outpouring of help, love, and compassion that is being exhibited across this country."

Leigh: Is there really going to be a war? Like, definitely?"

Dad: "Yes, there is going to be a war. It's not going to be like Vietnam or WWII. It is going to be like I described above. We have to stop them now or they will try building nukes and making chemical weapons. But don't worry. It is very unlikely it is going to affect you or me."

Leigh: "Do they even have the means to do that?"

Dad: "They are trying to do all those things. I don't think they can now, but that is why we have to stop them. Once this country is aroused and united, it is tough to stop. What you and your friends can do is be a voice of inclusion, not exclusion; be a voice of reason and compassion; be a voice of diversity; be a voice of hope and not despair. Make sure no students offend any students of color on your campus. Stand up for them. If there is anything to be learned by this, it is that our lives hang by such a fragile thread as spaceship earth hurtles through the universe at thousands of miles an hour, and we never know when that fickle finger of fate will strike and cut that thread."

Leigh: "Thanks, Dad."

Dad: "All that is important is our family, friends, and community. You, me, all your friends can fight back by volunteering, working in a homeless shelter, working in a soup kitchen, making this spaceship earth a better place. And yes, one person can make a difference. Look at those guys who fought the terrorists on that plane in PA. They prevented it from crashing into Washington DC. They knew they were going down but decided to do something about it. They are all heroes and saved thousands of lives."

Leigh: "Yes, they did."

Dad: "So you and your friends should not wonder what contribution you can each make. You can all do plenty. And each time one of us reaches out to help the sick, the poor, the oppressed, the hungry, or those in nursing homes, we are creating tiny ripples of hope. And pretty soon, these ripples of hope are crisscrossing the United States, from Durham, NH, from Harwich, MA, from Danbury, Ct, from Seguin, TX, from Fishers Island, NY, and from Plattsburgh, NY, and pretty soon these thousands of ripples of hope will become a giant wave that will knock down the walls of hate and desperation and hunger and poverty and racism in this great country of ours. Few of us can change the course of history, but we can make our home town, our community, our neighborhood, our home, a better place. There is a beautiful, sharp, smart, young lady who is a sophomore at UNH who already has generated many ripples of hope in her short lifetime, and I know there will be many more."

Leigh: "Thanks, Dad!"

And Then Some More

Always say "please."

Always say "thank you."

Always hold the door for the person behind you.

Always write thank you notes.

Always write a sympathy card with a personal note when a friend or co-worker loses a close family member.

When making a turn, always use your signal light before you turn.

Pay the toll for the person behind you once in a while.

When you go on a hike or walk, pick up a piece of trash. Leave the place cleaner than when you found it. Take only memories, and leave only footprints.

When someone moves in next to you—your house, apartment, condo, whatever—bring them a bottle of wine or champagne with a card to welcome them to the neighborhood.

Learn the names of all the folks you come in contact with and learn a little about each of them—Whether it's the janitor, the cafeteria folks, the security guards, the cleaning crew, the receptionist, the nursing home aids, and all the people who provide us with the services we need. Every one of them has a story and has hopes and dreams.

Say "hello" or "good morning" to everyone you meet or pass.

Give someone a compliment or congratulate him on something nice that happened in his life.

Do something nice for someone, and don't tell her.

Don't use your cell phone while driving or in public places like restaurants, libraries, book stores, and so on.

Always turn on your car lights when driving in the the snow or rain, and always clear the snow off your car before driving it.

Don't be rude or inconsiderate to anyone. There's too much negativity all around.

Pay for a meal at a restaurant for someone you don't know.

Watch *Extreme Makeover, Home Edition*—This is not just a TV show, but it's about home and inspiration and the triumph of the human spirit.

When you are at a red light and it changes to green, look quickly both ways to make sure someone is not running the light. It is better to be safe than dead right.

Grow a garden.

Recycle all your cans, bottles, and newspapers.

Start a compost pile.

Vote.

Dress up once in a while. Business casual and nonbusiness casual have gotten out of hand.

And always remember, don't ever eat yellow snow.

Epilogue

"Well, Fran," you're probably saying, "These Five Words are all well and good, but I've heard and read many different kinds of advice. How do I know that following these words will pay off and bring me success in life?" That's a good question.

Let me tell you a short story about a young man who grew up in a small town on Cape Cod many years ago. He didn't live in the fanciest house, and his family didn't have the biggest car. His family didn't have a lot of money, either. His SAT scores were only so-so, and his IQ wasn't anything great. He graduated in the middle of his high school class and in the bottom 5 percent of his college class. When he was in high school, his guidance counselor told his parents he shouldn't take French because he stuttered too much and he wouldn't be good with languages. And he was so nervous being an altar boy that he actually cried when his father dropped him off at mass because he was nervous about being in front of so many people.

After college graduation, he needed a job because he was getting married a few months later. He finally got one on his twenty-sixth interview, but it wasn't the job he applied for. He didn't qualify for that one, but they had a lower-level job that paid less money, and he needed work, so he took it.

And no matter what he did from then on, he applied these Five Words to everything he did—at work, in the community, at church, in the neighborhood, and in his home. And now many years later, he has the most beautiful wife, three wonderful children, and a really nice house and yard. He has retired from a high-level job with a major computer company where he made a very good salary. He has the respect and admiration of his family, friends, co-workers, and peers. And he has given speeches in front of hundreds of people.

And this man did all of the above because he applied these Five Words to everything he did. I think you know who I am talking about. He is the guy who wrote this book. Godspeed to you all.

"There comes a time when all the cosmic tumblers
have clicked into place and the universe opens itself up
for a few seconds to show you what's possible."

Ray Kinsella quoting Terrance Mann in the movie *Field of Dreams*